BUCKFAST
IN BYGONE DAYS
Memories and photographs of an
old Devon village

BUCKFAST
IN BYGONE DAYS
Memories and photographs of an old Devon village

Hilary Beard

DEVON BOOKS

First published in Great Britain in 1991 by Devon Books

British Library Cataloguing-in-Publication Data
Beard, Hilary
Buckfast in bygone days.
I. Title
942.35

ISBN 0-86114-872-X

Devon Books
397 Topsham Road
EXETER EX2 6HD (0392) 873215

Designed for Devon Books by
Topics Visual Information
397 Topsham Road
EXETER EX2 6HD (0392) 876800

THE COVER PHOTOGRAPH

There are those who say Buckfast never was a 'proper' village – and there are those who lived there in the past who will hotly deny this!

The scene shown is what could be said to be the heart of the village. In the Barracks, the building adjacent to the arch, several families lived in flats, and two families in Southgate Cottages, on the left. Beyond the arch was the village post office with its resident postmaster (the last one there being Mr Gilbert Petherick), Abbey Court Cottages, the Church of England School, Abbey Farm, Gatehouse Cottages, the Methodist Chapel, the temporary Catholic Church, and Northgate Cottages.

Just out of the picture on the left is St Mary's Convent School and, close by, a small bungalow. Opposite the School were the three rows of cottages known as New Buildings which branched off Gasworks Lane. On the gasworks premises was a substantial, detached, stone-built house where the managers lived.

The village shop, Bezzells, is next to the arch (on the left). In the centre of the picture is The Working Men's Institute, which at the time was also used as the Sunday School. The Institute was demolished in October 1991.

It is difficult to imagine today that within a stone's throw of this scene there were two schools, two places of worship, a village shop, recreation hall and village post office, along with a hundred or so residents (excluding the monks). Now, about six people live in the same area.

The little boy standing against the cottage is Redvers ('Jeddy') King. The girl is Winnie Lewis (later Crook) holding her brother Victor. The little girl standing next to them is Olive King. The horse and cart coming through the arch in the distance is believed to be from Northwood. The horse 'Fanny' is being driven by Tom Lewis, father of Winnie and Victor. Unfortunately the group with the pram can't be identified, though the girl with the white pinafore could be Maud Baker (later Emmett).

Though this photograph, originally on a postcard, is quite rare (it was taken in 1908), the author was extremely fortunate to be given two copies, one from Reg Crook and one from David Evans of Bourneville who discovered it in a Birmingham market!

Typeset by Exe Valley Imageset, Exeter.
Printed and bound by BPCC Wheaton Ltd, Exeter

CONTENTS

ACKNOWLEDGEMENTS

I am grateful to everyone who has helped me in any way with the production of this book, especially to those who have provided photographs, the selection of which has not been easy. All the photographs are individually credited apart from those in my family collection.

I am particularly indebted to the following people for the specialised help and advice: The Abbot and Community of Buckfast Abbey; Stewart Brown, archaeologist; Devon Books (in particular Simon Butler and Andy Jones – my last minute alterations surely drove them mad!); John Dutfield, Managing Director of Buckfast Spinning Company Ltd; James L. Hardy, Marketing Director of The House of Hardy Ltd, Alnwick; Brian Milsom of the Gas Historical Society, British Gas plc, Keynsham; Charles Coulton Stewart, former co-owner of Bulley Cleaves Quarry.

Finally my very special thanks to Reg Crook for all his practical advice and constructive criticism while helping me compile this book – and for typing the manuscript (several times!).

FOREWORD

I was born and brought up in Buckfast, my family having lived at Northwood for over a century.

The Beards were a local farming family from Widecombe and can be traced back for three hundred years. In the latter half of the last century my great grandfather, Thomas Lewis, rented what was known as Abbey Farm (the south wing of the Guest Hall), now in the process of being restored. Elizabeth, his daughter (my grandmother), was born at Abbey Farm. Annie Lewis, my great aunt, lived there until about 1938.

I was educated locally and later held a variety of interesting appointments, including working in Tenerife, children's homes, hotels and nursing homes, before I joined the Police Force, working in the Somerset and Avon area for almost ten years.

I never forgot my roots and returned 'home' as often as work would permit. Finally, until ill health forced my retirement, I worked in the local community for ten years as a nursing auxiliary, always taking the opportunity to talk to elderly local people, encouraging them to describe life in the old days.

Northwood
Buckfast
October 1991

A nineteenth century map – Buckfastleigh is marked but not Buckfast on Ordnance Survey maps of the period.

INTRODUCTION

In 1981 a pictorial history of Buckfastleigh, compiled by E. J. Beer, was published. It showed past scenes of life in the town, and some of the characters who helped create its history. I felt I would like to put together a similar book about Buckfast, my main aim being to preserve some of its previously unpublished photographs and soon-to-be-forgotten facts. The alterations that have and are still taking place have changed the landscape in such a way, that it will soon be very difficult to remember what the village used to look like.

Primarily this book is for the local people and their descendants. People, who like me, probably didn't know some of the facts in the history and guide books. I hope I have highlighted some of the more interesting anecdotes to go with the photographs.

I am very conscious that there are many areas of information about Buckfast that I have not included; but mainly I concentrated on the photographs that I had, providing informative captions to go with them. Also, I did not wish to repeat the information already contained in the books and guides specifically about the Abbey.

Having named nearly all the people in the photographs, I am hoping that with the increasing interest in genealogy, the descendants of Buckfast people will have an added bonus when they return to Buckfast to research their family history – a photograph to go with their names and dates.

Finally, though I have done my best to check details where possible, I apologise for any inaccuracies I have missed.

The Dart near Buckfastleigh

The
Origins of Buckfast

The name Buckfast is believed to have come from the Anglo-Saxon word Bucfaesten, meaning 'The fastness, or stronghold of the deer'. For centuries herds of deer roamed the slopes of Dartmoor, sheltering in the wooded valleys and drinking from the moorland streams and rivers. The village of Buckfast lies on the west bank of the River Dart, just below Hembury Woods – an ideal natural habitat for the deer. Though no herds of wild deer now remain in the area, there is ample evidence of their existence, probably up until the beginning of this century. Local people say that during the First World War, so much woodland was cut down for pit props, that the few remaining deer disappeared because they had no 'cover'.

In his book *One Hundred Years On Dartmoor*, William Crossing states that in the eighteenth century, the deer did much injury to the crops on the borders of the moor. He also writes that as far as recorded, 1780 was the year in which the last deer was killed by an organised pack of hounds (see page 12).

In the nearby village of Holne is a thirteenth-century church, which contains an early sixteenth-century pulpit, decorated with eight panels; each one being painted with shields of heraldic arms. One such panel shows the arms of the Abbey of Buckfast – which then possessed some land in the area. Today this coat of arms remains virtually unchanged – a stag's head with the crozier of an abbot. Present day visitors to the Abbey can see many examples of it.

The first written record of a monastic settlement at Buckfast is a confirmation by King Canute dated 1018. At that time all monasteries in England followed the Benedictine Rule. They were virtually the only sources of learning and teaching, as well as houses of prayer. Though there is no evidence it is probable that the village of Buckfast was originally a hamlet beside the Abbey.

In 1136 the Abbey was granted by King Stephen to the monastery at Savigny in France. Savignac houses were merged with the Cistercians in 1147. Under the Cistercians the monastery was completely rebuilt. The present Abbey Church is built on those same foundations.

The Cistercians were noted agriculturists, and under them the monks at Buckfast would have cleared the dense woodland and cultivated the surrounding land. Recent archaeological excavations bear this out. What was known (to the local residents) as 'Abbey Meadow' and is now the Abbey car park, was excavated in 1982 and found to have been originally covered in woodland, cleared in the thirteenth century.

This meadow probably provided sheltered pasture for stock brought down from the moors in the winter. Buckfast Abbey is only a

Deer killed in Brook Wood at the turn of the century.
(Courtesy of the late Mrs F. Orsman)

The couple in this photograph are Mr and Mrs MacOwen. Mrs MacOwen was believed to have been a housekeeper at nearby Brook Manor, and Mr MacOwen was Clerk of Works for the building of the Venford Dam (Paignton Water Works) which was completed in 1907. Brook Woods are about two miles from Buckfast. Until recently at least twelve sets of antlers and stags heads hung on the walls of Brook Manor. An inscription under one of them read 'This stag was roused in Brook Wood after a very fine chase of 5½ hours, by the hounds of Bidlake Herring Esq., September 17th 1780.'

Mr Knight, a self-employed sculptor, carving the Abbey coat of arms in the Abbey Church.
(Courtesy of Buckfast Abbey)

The Coat of Arms can be seen just below the balcony at the west entrance.

few miles from the edge of Dartmoor, where the monks kept sheep and cattle. Prior to the first Plague (1348) there was always a lay-brother living and working on the moor, looking after the stock there. The last lay-brother to live and work there was a Brother Henry Walbrook. In 1956, the remains of a medieval homestead were discovered on the site of the present Avon Dam on Dean Moor. This was thought to be the homestead occupied by Brother Henry Walbrook and other lay-brothers from Buckfast Abbey.

In the thirteenth century, the Abbot of Buckfast was admitted as a member of the Totnes Merchants Guild, thus ensuring the Abbey's involvement both socially and economically in South Devon. By the fourteenth century, Buckfast, like other monastic houses, was trading in wool with the Florentines – Totnes, Dartmouth and Kingsbridge being convenient ports for Buckfast.

In 1983, archaeological excavations revealed that a monastic guest hall, opposite the west front of the Abbey, was first built in the twelfth century, but rebuilt on a larger scale around 1300 to become one of the largest guest halls in the country. Presumably this was necessary so that the Buckfast monks could provide hospitality for the large number of travellers and merchants using the important route leading south-west from Exeter.

The guest quarters were again enlarged in the early fifteenth century, by the addition of a south wing – known until recently as 'Abbey Farm', and used as a tea room until 1982.

At the time of writing the guest hall walls and buildings that remain are in urgent need of repair and restoration. Restoration has begun on the south wing.

At the time of the Dissolution, the Abbey Church buildings and some land were granted to a Sir Thomas Denis (or Denys), on 25 February 1539. The lead was stripped from the roof, and the bells were sold to the people of Buckfastleigh. Those bells, though recast, are still rung from the parish church on the hill. Gradually the Abbey Church and buildings became ruins – local people used the stone for building. There are some very fine barns in the locality. For many years Buckfast was known as 'Buckfast Denis', and by a strange quirk of fate when the monks returned to Buckfast in 1882, their first superior was a Dom Stephen Denis.

The Abbey and buildings remained in a ruinous state until the end of the eighteenth century, when a Samuel Berry, owner of the adjacent woollen mill purchased the site, levelled the ruins and built a mansion, completed in 1806. The mansion house still stands and can be seen today between the Abbey Church and the monastery. The only part of the medieval ruins that Samuel Berry left standing was the twelfth century vault, which he incorporated into the mansion as cellars, and the fifteenth century Abbots Tower. The mansion was built with stones from the old ruins. Some years later Berry was bankrupt, and the mansion passed through other hands before it was acquired by a community of Benedictine monks in 1882.

In contrast to the ruination of the Abbey, following the Dissolution, the woollen industry continued to prosper in the area. Could it be that some of the 'pensioned off' monks remained in the area and continued to use their expertise in the woollen trade? It flourished in the 17th and 18th centuries and it is recorded that as late as 1878 there were five mills connected with the woollen industry in the parish of Buckfastleigh alone (Buckfast being in the parish). The industry also flourished in the nearby market towns of Ashburton and Totnes.

The industry gradually declined and the sole survivors today are the Buckfastleigh Fellmongery (where sheepskins are treated), and the Buckfast Spinning Company, a subsidiary of Axminster Carpets Ltd, which is now on the site of what is known as Lower

The old stone wall at Northgate Arch.

Parts of this wall are believed to be twelfth century. At that time the gateway would have been much larger and connected by groined vaulting. Some protrusions which formed part of the vaulting can still be seen today. It is possible that there was a small chapel above the arch, as in many Cistercian Abbeys at that time. This is one of the few remaining examples of the early Cistercian architecture at Buckfast.

Archaeological excavations, 1982

These show remains of medieval walls. Those seen in the centre (on the right) date from the thirteenth century and (the left) the fifteenth century. These walls supported buildings thought to be workshops, animal houses etc. The Northgate can be seen top right.

Avon Dam, Dean Moor 1989.
(*Courtesy Barrington Weekes*)

The severe drought in 1989 reduced the water level to such an extent that it revealed the ruins of what is believed to be the medieval homestead of Brother Henry Walbrook.

Mills, formerly Berry's Mill. There were two mills on the one site, the blanket mill being known as 'Little Mill'. The other mill was mainly involved in the making of navy serges. The work at the Buckfast Spinning Company (sorting, washing, treating, dying and spinning woollen yarn for the world famous Axminster Carpets), could be said to be the continuation of that woollen industry, laid down centuries ago by the Cistercian monks at Buckfast.

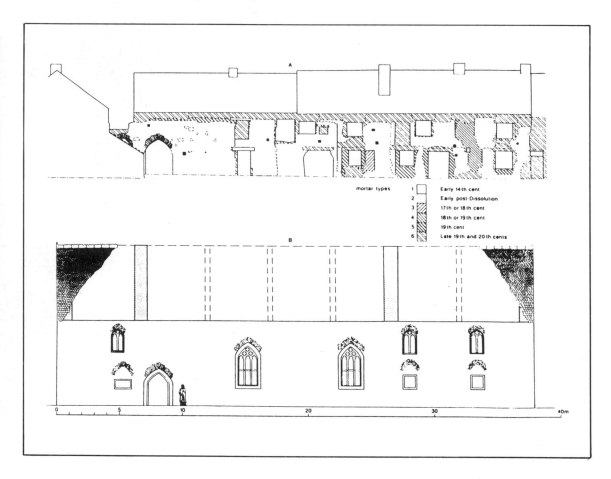

		mortar types	
1			Early 14th cent
2			Early post-Dissolution
3			17th or 18th cent
4			18th or 19th cent
5			19th cent
6			Late 19th and 20th cents

Diagram of the guest hall – facing the west front of the Abbey Church.
(*Courtesy of Mr Stewart Brown*)

This building was formerly known as Gate House Cottages – the Wesleyan Chapel being to the right of the picture, and 'Abbey Farm' to the left. This diagram was produced by the archaeologists led by Stewart Brown, in 1983. Part 'A' shows the building as it is today, the fine doorway on the left can still be clearly seen. Part 'B' shows the guest hall as it would have been – with a very much higher roof. This guest hall did not have a chimney – heat would have been provided by an open fire in the centre of the hall, the smoke escaping through a louvre above the rafters. The arched doorway can still be seen today, as in the photo on page 16.

Building known as 'Abbey Farm'.
(Courtesy of Mr R. Crook)
This building was originally the guest hall complex, built in the fifteenth century.

Contemporary view of part of the remains of the guest hall.
(Courtesy of J. Beard)

A print of the Mansion House built by John Berry in 1806.
The present Monastery and Abbey Church were built around this imposing edifice.

The Monks Return to Buckfast (and Fundraising)

Annie, Annie! Where's Annie?' 'ers up watching they monks again'. Annie, the unmarried daughter of Tom and Mary Ann Lewis, was living in Abbey Farm opposite the Abbey grounds, when, at the end of October, 1882, the first party of monks arrived to set up their monastic home in the mansion house.

Thirty men, speaking a foreign tongue, dressed in long black flowing robes and with 'funny haircuts' (tonsures) – no wonder Annie spent much of her time 'watching they monks'. They were 'Papists' – coming to live in a village where most of the inhabitants were of the Protestant or Wesleyan faith. Annie was not the only one who watched 'they monks' – for it is recorded in the Abbey annals of that time, that the mill workers would spend their lunch hour, climbing the walls hoping to see the monks!

What an impact they must have had on the village, where the majority of inhabitants worked in the woollen mills, or on the land, for six days a week, and went to church or chapel on the seventh.

In 1880 the French government had passed anti-clerical laws. Monasteries were suppressed and their inhabitants expelled, sometimes by force. The monks who came to Buckfast were some of the victims of those laws, previously members of the Benedictine Abbey of La Pierre-qui-Vire. They had taken part in a 'sit in' when it was their turn to be evicted! Each monk locked himself in his cell, thus compelling the evicting forces to smash each individual door, and drag the 'miscreant' monk out. After leaving France, they sought refuge in this country at St Augustines Priory (later Abbey) in Ramsgate. It was there that Father Adam Hamilton joined them – the only English speaking monk. He was a genial and scholarly man, liked and respected by everyone who came into contact with him. He was later to write the *History of Buckfast Abbey*, published in 1906.

Following a succession of fortuitous events, the monks took up residence in the vacant mansion house on the old Abbey site. Father Adam soon had the support of the local people, who were able to help the impoverished monks in practical ways. A Buckfastleigh baker, John Hunt, provided bread, free of charge for two years. In the early days, the monks used packing cases as tables and chairs and ate in relays because there was not sufficient cutlery! Following the Benedictine Rule of self sufficiency, the monks took it in turn to do the cooking – sometimes with dire results!

Their first priority on arrival at Buckfast, was to have a temporary church built, and this was completed in 1884.

However the real hope of the Buckfast community was to rebuild an Abbey on the ancient site. It is said that the original foundations were discovered soon after their

Abbot Boniface Natter, with Bishop Graham (of Plymouth) and the Community at Buckfast
c. 1903 (Courtesy of Buckfast Abbey)

arrival by a monk digging in the vegetable garden. A young and enthusiastic architect, Frederick Walters had already drawn up one design, but it would have been in the 'wrong place' – so now he was asked to design the Abbey Church using the original foundations. This he did, and the Buckfast Abbey we see today is the result of that design first conceived at the end of the last century.

Abbot Natter is seated fourth from the right, next to Bishop Graham wearing his Biretta. Father Adam Hamilton is second from the left in the front row (with walking stick). Fourth from the left in the front row is Father Edmund who served in the army of Napoleon III, and was nearly a hundred years of age when he died at Buckfast in 1937. In the far right of the back row is Father Dunstan who used to say Mass for the prisoners at Princetown on a Sunday. This entailed setting off at 3am, on foot, after Matins, for the long and solitary walk across the moors. Also seated in the front row third from the right is Father Winfrid Rechtsteiner, second right is Father Mellitus Hauler, and on the far right

Father Wilfrid Schneider, the first Catholic parish priest of Totnes since the Reformation. The community was raised to the status of Abbey in 1902, when, at the age of 36, Father Boniface Natter was elected the first Abbot of Buckfast since the Reformation. He was, like Father Adam Hamilton, very popular with the local community. One local person was heard to say 'he knew no side'! He too had been inspired with the idea of rebuilding an Abbey at Buckfast, but money – or lack of it, was the problem.

The fascinating vision of a restored Abbey Church appealed to many. Soon after the monks arrival, a national committee was founded, whose members were prominent Catholics of their time. They themselves were benefactors of the Buckfast Community and encouraged others with fundraising activities. The Ninth Lord Clifford of Chudleigh, whose ancestral home is Ugbrooke, was particularly generous. He was mainly responsible for the building of the south and east wings and cloisters of the monastery, whilst the Hon. Charles Clifford (later 11th Baron Clifford) had the north cloister built in the 1920s.

Mabel, 9th Lady Clifford, paid for central heating to be installed in the monks' cells, and possibly in other parts of the monastery. In recognition of the Clifford's generosity Abbot Vonier drew up a 'letter of commitment' which said that as long as there shall be Benedictines at Buckfast, Mass should be said at Ugbrooke on twelve months of the year.

Temporary church.
This was designed by Bishop Vaughan of Plymouth, and solemnly inaugurated on the 25 March (Lady Day) 1884.

Interior of the temporary church.
The actual building was carried out by Samuel Furneaux of Buckfastleigh, whilst the woodwork, benches of the nave and the monks' choir stalls, was executed by Aaron Wakeham, also of Buckfastleigh.

Abbey Farm, photographed around the time of the Monks return to the Abbey.

The returning monks would have been familiar with this scene, taken *c.* 1890. Mr Dyer is the postman talking to Mr Thomas Lewis at the door, while Mary Ann Lewis (the 'Annie' mentioned at the start of this chapter) stands at the head of the pony, possibly the postman's?

Fund-raising at Buckfast *c.* 1903.

For many years, prior to the First World War, the annual summer bazaars held in the meadows near the Abbey site, were a major event in the locality, the proceeds from these bazaars going towards the rebuilding of the Abbey church. This strange flotilla, pictured on the 'Weir Pool' of the River Dart at Buckfast, was one of the principal attractions. The 'boats', for want of a better word, were built by John Beard of Northwood Farm, mainly from cider barrels. The Buckfastleigh town band would march in to open the proceedings and they played late into the evening. There was dancing in the meadows, and the river was lit up with hundreds of coloured lights – some of them floating on the water (this was done by placing 'night lights' on little wooden floats). There were all the usual attractions, including various stalls, cream teas, bowling for the pig, rifle shooting, etc.

In the boat nearest the camera can be seen a monk holding the flag pole. This was Abbot Natter, the first Abbot of Buckfast since 1539. On the right is John Beard who made the boats, and on the left is his wife Elizabeth. The lady in the centre is believed to be Miss Fifine Herring-Mason, a professional singer whose fine voice was part of the bazaar entertainment, particularly when she sang from a candlelit boat on the river.

Abbot Natter was to drown tragically on the 4 August 1906, when the ship, *Sirio*, in which he was travelling, was wrecked off the coast of Spain. His travelling companion, Father Anscar Vonier survived and was subsequently elected the next Abbot of Buckfast – and it was he who was to carry out the dream of Abbot Natter – to rebuild an Abbey Church at Buckfast on the twelfth century foundations. Anscar Vonier was only thirty years of age when he was elected. Under his forceful personality fundraising took off with a vengeance!

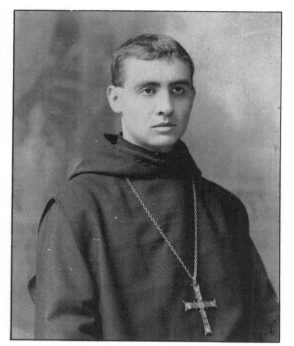

The young Abbot Vonier, probably taken shortly after his election in 1906.

Leaflet advertising the bazaar in 1909.
(*Courtesy of Mrs G. Henle*)
The letters at the foot of the leaflet are the initials of *Ut In Omnibus Glorificetur Deus* – 'That God may be glorified in all things', from Chapter 57 of the Rule of Saint Benedict.

Some leading personalities at the bazaar held on the 14 July, 1914.
(*Courtesy of Buckfast Abbey*)

In the centre from left to right – Father Kirk of Paignton, Abbot Vonier and Father Bernard Vaughan.

Behind the scenes at the bazaar *c.* 1903.
(Courtesy of Mr R. Crook)

These helpers had probably just finished clearing up behind the tea tent. The name E. B. Tope, tent maker of Hoe Street, Plymouth, can just be deciphered on the end of the tent. This firm was founded in 1880 and was in existence for one hundred years before being renamed, in 1980, Black and Edgington. The people in the photo are from left to right: Mrs Maria Crook, Mrs McCarthy, Mrs Foster, Charlie Foster and Bill Chivall.

Buckfast Villas in Northwood Lane *c.* 1890.

Some of these villas were built by people who later became benefactors of the Abbey Church. One of them 'St Benets', not yet built in this photo, was used to accommodate the Sisters of Charity when they first came to Buckfast in 1901. The present convent house not being built until 1911.

To the left can be seen the mill chimney stack, the north wing of the Monastery, and the Mansion House. The two fields are now occupied by the monks' private cemetery. The Abbey preparatory school, and the present apiary would be to the extreme right.

Serving teas – Abbey tea gardens *c.* 1930.
Miss Retallack, standing, in the white coat, serving customers. She, together with other ladies of the parish, decided that the increasing numbers of visitors needed refreshment. They were all volunteers, and any profits went towards the building fund.

The Abbey choir stalls under construction *c.* 1930.
(*Courtesy of Mr R. Crook*)
The cost of this work was donated by Miss Retallack, a parishioner of Buckfast.

PICTORIAL RECORD
OF THE
REBUILDING OF THE ABBEY CHURCH

**Brothers restoring Buckfast Abbey
foundations, 1904.**

The Brothers dressing stone.
This photo was taken prior to the First World
War. From left to right an unnamed French lay
brother, Brothers Ignatius Birk (one of the
principal builders), Anthony Fisher, and
Fridolin Rolf.

    At the outbreak of the First World War most
of the community were Germans and were
confined to the Abbey grounds for the
duration of the war. Friends and neighbours
helped to conduct any 'outside business'.

The laying of the foundation stone, 1907.
(*Courtesy of Buckfast Abbey*)
The Orator at the ceremony was Father
Bernard Vaughan a celebrated Edwardian
society preacher. He had six brothers who
became priests, and six sisters who entered
convents. One brother was Cardinal Herbert
Vaughan, Archbishop of Westminster from
1892 to 1903.

**Another scene of the Brothers dressing the
Bath stone.**
Dressing the stone was found to be a time
consuming process, and after 1917 the stone

was delivered already dressed. The monk with the handsaw is believed to be Martin Henle, and one of the principal builders, Brother Hilarion, is on the extreme right.

Brothers at work – prior to the First World War.
Note the block and chain, and the monk on the right controlling it.

A View of the temporary west front.
This was completed in 1922 enabling the new Abbey Church to be used for worship for the first time. The marks from the main doors seen in this picture can still be seen half way down the main aisle. It was to take another ten years before the Abbey Church was finally completed and consecrated. (The temporary west front had then to be demolished – which apparently proved a more difficult task than the building of it. Such was the quality of Brother Peter's masonry.)

The blessing of the Abbey Church 3 August, 1922.

Starting the new west front 1 May, 1925.
The man with the beard, leaning against the rail, is Walter Weeks, a former proprietor of the Sun Inn at Buckfastleigh. He was also a glazier, and was to be responsible for putting in many of the windows of the Abbey Church. He took a great interest in the building, and some local people recall how he used to climb the ladders leading to the scaffolding closely followed by his little terrier dog. On the extreme right is Brother Peter Schrode, the master mason, with him is Brother Hilarion and in the foreground is Brother Ignatius.

These three lay brothers, together with Father Richard Dillenz (not in the photo) were the four principal builders – working from dawn to dusk from 1907 to 1937.

The construction provided work for several local craftsmen. Petherbridge and Sons, the local ironmongers and blacksmith of Buckfastleigh, provided the ironwork for the windows. This was made by George Foot, a farrier. Stanley Harris, later to become the local plumber, helped to fix the rainwater pipes, while Hoskings & Sons made nearly all the oak doors and the wooden supports needed in the construction of stone arches.

Sorting the building stones *c.* 1928.
It is said that Abbot Vonier loved trees and he took some persuading before he agreed to the felling of this large poplar. The monk in the foreground, Brother Hilarion, is sorting the building stones. The white Bathstone arrived by the wagonload at Buckfastleigh railway station and would be stockpiled there. Every day, during his lunch hour, Brother Peter walked to the station and numbered the stones he would need the following day. Though most of the 'building monks' handled most of the stone, it is said that Brother Hilarion handled *every* stone. His duty was to stockpile the stones, already numbered, and send them up to the builders in the correct order. The stone came from Monkspark Quarry at Corsham in Wiltshire.

The Brothers at work *c.* **1929.**

Brothers Matthias, Peter, Paschal and an unknown brother. From time to time men would 'try their vocation' for the religious life – but decided it was not for them, and leave before making lifelong vows, and return to the outside world. What interesting memories some of these temporary building monks must have taken with them.

Buckfast Abbey Church. The west front in the course of erection, 1929.

About this time extra labour was needed in order to meet the Consecration deadline of 1932. The new workers included Harold Austin, Sammy and John Hayman, and Fred Lane.

Originally the red sandstone, required for the roof of the nave, was quarried at Ugbrooke, Chudleigh, but this was proving to be expensive and time consuming. In order to speed up the work these men helped erect what one monk described as 'synthetic sandstone' – in fact, coloured cement.

Note the enormous pole ladders on the left which would have taken several men to erect.

Completing the west front, 1929.
Brothers Ignatius, Peter, Paschal and Conrad.

Consecration of the Abbey Church 25 August, 1932.

This ceremony attracted nationwide interest. Pope Pius XI commissioned Cardinal Bourne, Archbishop of Westminster, to perform the ceremony of dedication, and for this occasion appointed him 'Papal Legate'. The village was beflagged, with festoons and banners from Dartbridge up to and including the Abbey Church. It was estimated that there were 1000 people inside the church, and over 2000 outside – even though the ceremony took many hours. In this picture Cardinal Bourne can be seen during part of the consecration service at the West Front. The police constable is thought to be P.C. Gould.

Monks working on the Abbey Tower *c.* 1934.

Here we see the builders constructing the turret, or staircase to the top. Brothers Paul and Peter, Father Richard Dillenz and Brother Paschal.

The Abbey Tower was not completed until 1938.

Abbot Vonier in his later years.

Abbot Vonier died on Boxing Day 1938. As he had been elected Abbot in 1906, he had been able to oversee the rebuilding of the Abbey Church from the foundations in 1907 to its final completion in 1938. The structure of the tower was actually completed in 1937 – but between then and 1938 each stone was pointed and cleaned as the scaffolding was dismantled.

Brother Peter carrying in the scaffolding after the exterior of the Abbey Church had been completed.

Probably taken in August 1932, prior to the consecration on the twenty-fifth of that month.

To many the name of Brother Peter is synonymous with the rebuilding of Buckfast Abbey Church. In 1901 Abbot Leander Lemoine – the then acting Superior at Buckfast Priory (it was not raised to the status of Abbey until 1902) decided to send a teenage monk to an Abbey in France to learn masonry. This was Brother Peter Schrode. He received less than two years training, and then returned to Buckfast.

On being elected Abbot in 1906, Abbot Vonier almost immediately placed the young Brother Peter in charge of the rebuilding. He was only 23 years of age, and had no other experienced or qualified masons to help him. In fact, he had to teach other monks his own skills in order that, together, they could re-build the Abbey Church.

The first stone was laid in January 1907. From then on until 1938, when the Abbey was completed, Brother Peter was in charge, working closely with Frederick Walters the Architect, who until his death in 1932 came down regularly from London to check the progress of the building work. Fortunately, the then Great Western Railway provided good connections to Buckfastleigh. One can imagine the sense of anticipation the architect felt every time he made that journey, looking forward to seeing his plans gradually taking shape.

Brother Peter was a remarkable monk, largely responsible for an exceptional building feat, yet in his latter years he would stand quietly at the back of 'his church', unsung and unfeted. The crowds of visitors sweeping past him little realised that this unassuming monk had played such a major part in the rebuilding of the Abbey Church.

Following its completion in 1938, Brother Peter took an active interest in all other building and maintenance work up until his death in 1975, at the age of 92.

A LIGHT HEARTED
LOOK AT LADDERS AND LEVERAGE
LADDERS? WHAT LADDERS?

What would a present day Safety Inspector say about the monks' method of transport, to and from the building site.

Welcome aboard. (*Courtesy of Buckfast Abbey*) Brother Paschal waiting to be hauled aboard by Brother Peter. This method was commonly used by the builders. Note only one foot 'secure' in the chain loop, and also the complete lack of safety rails on the platform. In this scene they were working about fifty feet up.

Working on a west front pinnacle.
(*Courtesy of Buckfast Abbey*)
Brother Paschal contemplates a newly arrived stone. It must be time for a coffee break (it is interesting to note that he is standing next to a ladder).

Going down? (*Courtesy of Buckfast Abbey*)

He did decide to have a coffee break. This was a 'safe' way down because he had a 'platform for both feet'. Brother Hilarion who operated the hoist from ground level was a noted 'expert' in this field. The descent, in particular, was undertaken at frightening speed until the bucket, man or wheelbarrow was but a few feet from the ground. The brake was then applied with a vengeance. Whoever or what-ever was coming down came to a shuddering halt and the remaining few feet taken in a sedate fashion. Brother Hilarion and his hoist always drew a crowd of onlookers and he must have been photographed many times. He could truly be described as the 'gentle giant' of the building group. He used to mix all the cement by hand, no task for a weakling. His main tool was the Devon shovel – peculiar to this region. It had a heart shaped blade on a long curved handle, enabling one to work without bending the back, and the correct handle was very important. A local saying advised 'You gotta pick a shovel stick when you see 'un – else 'ees there gone'.

From time to time, it was inevitable, that accidents, or near misses would occur but they were remarkably few. One of the more potentially serious accidents is clearly recalled by Brother Paschal, who together with Brothers Peter and Placid Sa'ad were coming down together on the hoist. This was an exception to the normal practice of one at a time – but it was about 9.30am on a frosty morning and they were going for their coffee break. When Brother Hilarion applied the brake nothing happened and the three men crashed to the ground. One can imagine the look of horror on his face when he realised the brake was frozen solid – not having been operated pre-viously that day. Brother Sa'ad was taken to the local hospital and spent two weeks there being treated for a back injury (he had been sent to Buckfast to learn masonry with Brother Peter – one wonders if he ever employed the same method of trans-port when he returned to Jerusa-lem). Remarkably Brothers Peter and Paschal were uninjured. 'We had a few hours off, and then returned to work' says Brother Paschal laconically.

Following this accident Abbot Vonier forbade the practice of using the hoist instead of ladders. Whether this instruction was followed to the letter is doubtful.

RETURN TO BUCKFAST

SIR: Many years ago, I spent a few days touring with my parents in South Devon, and one particular outing on that holiday I have always remembered. So much so that while visiting Torquay recently, I decided to make a sentimental journey, a sort of pilgrimage. For, as a ten-year-old, I was taken to see Buckfast Abbey Church under construction and was invited by two of the brothers, working aloft, to join them as they laboured laying a course of stonework. Should he carry me up the wooden ladders, pick-a-back manner, asked my father? No, responded the builders. They would lower down a large wooden bucket in which I was to sit. So it was, and cautioned not to fidget but to "hold tight", I was gently hauled up by the monks to the place where they were working. Even now, I recall vividly gingerly stepping out of the "lift" and, while my father negotiated the system of ladders to join us, being shown round but kept well away from the edge of the scaffolding, way above terra-firma. One of the brothers demonstrated how to use a trowel and then persuaded me to have a go. What

youngster would refuse? In time I managed to lay sufficient mortar on the upper surface of a large stone then watched while one of a similar size was carefully lowered onto it. Thus, my tiny contribution to the building of the church duly completed, and the kindly brothers thanked, father and I returned, by the reverse procedure to earth.

With that impression so firmly etched on my mind, how can I describe seeing the completed building for the first time after so long an absence? Truly magnificent, isn't it, both within and without. The more so when one remembers how very few brother-tradesmen there were and the then lack of sophisticated building materials such as we know them today. I'm glad I made the journey for, having seen it through the eyes of a child, now, with more mature optics, I was privileged to see the whole. —JOE CASTLE, SHEFFIELD.

*Thousands of people visit Buckfast every year, but not many can say they helped to build it. Ed.

Letter from an onlooker.
(*Courtesy of* This England *magazine, 1976*)
One of the many onlookers remembers the days when, as a young boy, he was taken to see the building work in progress. The memory reflects the impression most onlookers must have had.

Builder in retirement, 1991.
Just to prove that our hoist riding Brother Paschal survived his hair-raising trips here is a recent photograph. He is the last of the 'building monks'.

WHY IS BUCKFAST ABBEY
A TOURIST ATTRACTION?

As a child I often asked myself this question. It is a modern building – not old and interesting, like some Churches. Now it is the top tourist attraction in Devon, attracting nearly half a million visitors every year.

It is through researching this book, that I have come to realise how Buckfast became a tourist attraction. In the last century there were not many Roman Catholics in this area. They were called Papists by many, a derogatory term. The mere fact that some foreign monks (mainly French originally and then German at the turn of the century) came to settle in Devonshire in 1882 was newsworthy in itself but, when at the beginning of the twentieth century they actually started rebuilding an old Abbey in the Medieval style – well this really caught the imagination.

Magazines and periodicals began to record the happenings at Buckfast, and by the nineteen twenties and thirties, the rebuilding of the Abbey Church, by a handful of monks had inspired the Nation. The local and national press reported the various stages of the rebuilding, which encouraged people to see for themselves this extraordinary sight – and so it was that Buckfast Abbey became a tourist attraction.

INDUSTRY

Up to the end of the nineteenth century Buckfast was part of a busy, prosperous industrial area, with several corn mills, iron foundry, tanneries, tin and copper mines, limestone quarries, lime kilns and, of course, the woollen mills at Ashburton, Buckfast and Buckfastleigh.

Berry's Mill or Lower Mills
This site is now part of the Buckfast Spinning Company Ltd. The mill used to dominate the village, with its huge chimney stack (demolished in 1979). In this photograph, taken about 1903, the site of the present Abbey Church is to the left of the stack. The mill was

famous for its blankets, and on the extreme right can be seen the 'racks' where they were dried as part of their finishing process. As recently as 1964, whilst under the ownership of the present Buckfast Spinning Company, over 4000 blankets were produced in a week, along with a large number of car rugs and carpet yarn. Due to the increasing use of cheaper synthetic blankets by competitors, and the advent of the continental quilt, it became uneconomical to continue production of these goods and the mill turned to producing yarn for Axminster carpets. These are 100 per cent wool – 95 per cent of that being from the British Isles. The British Woolmarketing Board until recently had a large store at Buckfastleigh, and much of the wool taken there by local farmers eventually ended up in Axminster carpets.

Buckfast, as well as being famous for its blankets, also produced a serge material which was much in demand by the Admiralty during both World Wars. The late Bill Coram, a former employee at Berry's Mill, recalled that prior to the First World War, a red material was produced, and referred to as 'Company Cloth'. It was exported to China! 'Collar checks' was another product woven in the mill, these being used to cover the padding of horse harness.

During the last war, as part of the 'war effort' Sea Boot Wool, a thick, oiled knitting wool, was produced and used for knitting long socks for seamen. The ladies of the village used to knit them, vying with each other to see who could knit the most pairs!

Camouflage nets were another product and due to all this extra work the woollen mills prospered during wartime, but were short of work during peacetime. However, under the present management, the mill has expanded and is now one of the foremost carpet yarn spinning mills in the country. The high quality yarn is used in the production of Axminster Carpets – now in world-wide demand, thus ensuring continuous work at Buckfast and resulting in an extension to the Mill in 1989.

In the foreground of the photograph is

Southpark Orchard, one of many such orchards in the area then producing apples for the local cider industry. There were pound houses (where apples were crushed to extract the juice) at Blackrock, Ware House, Pridhamsleigh, Dartbridge Road, plus many more in the parish. John Symons & Company had a bottling and distribution centre at Totnes, and a cider store in the Old Totnes Road at Buckfastleigh, where the juice was fermented in vats. It is recorded in Kellys Directory of 1850, that a one-acre orchard in the parish, produced 4000 gallons of cider; Symons used to boast that they made the best cider in the West Country. In pre-war days it sold at 9d (4½p) a quart. Although the village never had a public house, as such, there was in the late nineteenth century a cider house in what is now known to be the remains of the Abbey guest hall. It was popular with the mill workers during their lunch break – but following a serious accident, one afternoon when a worker lost an arm, these visits were forbidden by the mill owners.

On the extreme left of the photograph is the chimney stack of Higher Mill.

Footbridge over the River Dart, beside the Abbey c. 1890. (*Courtesy of Mr V. Gruitt*)
Known locally as the 'Clam Bridge', it was used for many years by the millworkers from Ashburton as a short cut to and from work.

When in full flood the river would rise above the bridge level, and one winter's evening, in the twenties, John Kingwell, an Ashburton millworker, was swept from the bridge and drowned.

In 1970 the bridge was destroyed by a great flood, and was replaced by a much larger construction a little upstream from the old site. It is interesting that in the background of this photograph a second camera and photographer can be seen.

Higher Mill, Buckfast.

Formerly a woollen mill, owned by the Hamlyn family of Buckfastleigh, it was sold, in 1922, to the Buckfastleigh Co-operative Wholesale Society who used it as a woollen store for their mill at Buckfastleigh, famous for its West of England serge. An unusual feature at the back of the building is a wooden launder, which carried water to the water wheel. The water came via a system of leats and streams from the nearby moors. Higher Mill is joined to the Lower Mills by a leat which passes under the road at Southgate arch. In the latter part of the nineteenth century there was lengthy litigation between the two mills involving the use of water. The Hamlyn's claimed that Messrs Berry were mis-using the water in such a way as to decrease the power of their water wheel. The level of water in dispute was only about 2 inches in depth – but enough to hamper the turning of the water wheel.

During the Second World War troops were billeted here. About 1950 the building was used as a plating works until 1989 when it was bought by Buckfast Abbey, who plan to use it in the production of their famous tonic wine.

NOTICE
HOIST, Doors fences or trapdoors must be kept shut. Any persons leaving them open will be subject a fine of ONE SHILLING

No one must use the Hoist, except those appointed by the Overlookers in each room.

Anyone breaking this rule will be subject to a fine of 2/6d

HAMLYN BROS

Inset: a facsimile of a notice found in the Higher Mill.

A soldier's artistry.
This cartoon was drawn on an interior wall of Higher Mill by a member of the 'Ox and Bucks' Regiment. Despite the passing years it can still be clearly seen today.

Buckfast *c.* 1910. (*Courtesy of Mrs V. Farquhar*)
A horse and wagon leaving Berry's Mill gates with a loom, on its way to take part in the Buckfastleigh carnival. Edward Willis, a foreman at Willcock's Engineering Works for forty-two years, is standing on the wagon, with Mr Steer at the horse's head. On the extreme right is Walter Wood who was the foreman of the serge weaving shed.

The fire engine and crew of Buckfast Lower Mill *c.* 1905. (*Courtesy of Miss J. Edworthy*)
Mr William Edworthy (centre) is holding the hose. At this time the mill was owned by Messrs Berry, and fire was a very real hazard in the old buildings, and several serious fires are recorded in the last hundred years. Lower Mill was burnt down in 1877, causing a loss of £40 000 and throwing 450 persons out of employment. No doubt telegrams were sent to Ashburton and Totnes for fire engines – for it is recorded that in 1882, when a 50 foot high rick of bark caught fire at the Buckfastleigh Tanyard, that this method of communication was used.

A household group at Kenwyn, Ashburton *c.* 1916. (*Courtesy of Mrs K. Shillabeer*)
The children are believed to be John, Ben, and Simon Berry with their nanny (centre). The gardener (rear right) is Mr James Shillabeer. Kenwyn and its neighbour known as Waverley Hall were built by the mill-owning Berry family.

A group of mill workers from Berry's Mill in the 1920s. (*Courtesy of Mrs S. Piper*)
The mill leat ran from the Abbey Weir Pool, through a meadow at the rear of Buckfast Abbey and into the woollen mills, whose property adjoins that of the Abbey, where it provided power and water for the cleaning process. The leat was cleaned every twelve months when the mill was closed for its annual holidays. This photograph was probably taken during such a week.

Another group of mill workers in the 1920s. (*Courtesy of Miss J. Edworthy*)
This scene is outside their Working Men's Institute, later to become St Mary's Parish Hall. Some of the workmen came from Buckfastleigh, and there are still people who can remember, as children, going to the local board school at Buckfastleigh, running home at lunchtime, only to grab a slice of bread and jam, and then having to take a hot meal out to their father at Berry's Mill. The Pathfields, a footpath by the present Buckfast Nursery, would be their

route. They then had to run back to school in time for their afternoon lessons.

In this group from left to right (up and down) are: Albert Knowling, Jack Cook, Billy Grute, Harold Burt, William Edworthy, Horace Wood, Charlie Foster, Adrian Chivall, Horace Chivall, Billy Mitchell, Billy Mugford, Leonard Prowse, Bill King (who lost his left arm in an accident at the mill), Jack Ham, Harry French and Jack Burt.

Accidents in the mill were not uncommon, and one notice, dated 21 May 1895 (the original is in Totnes Museum) read: 'Women, Young Persons and Children are strictly forbidden to clean any Machinery in motion or during Meal Hours. Hands disobeying this Notice are liable to instant dismissal. John Berry and Sons.' The men were obviously trusted!

A young girl called Kathleen Shillabeer from Ashburton crushed her hand in a loom (she was looking after an extra loom because someone was away sick). The nearest pony and trap was at the adjacent Abbey, where Brother Peter was working on the restoration. He administered 'First Aid' (sloe gin) and then drove her

to Ashburton Hospital for treatment.

Buckfast saying: 'Come 'ere and I'll knock the Ashburton man off your back' (said to anyone who was lazy). Ashburton people said the same of Buckfast men!

James and Jane Searle, 1880.

James Searle was a woolcomber and he and his wife lived at 'New Buildings'. These were three rows of cottages by the main entrance to the mill, built for the workers. Descendants of the Searle family still live in the area. Whites Directory of 1851 stated that there were three hundred woolcombers in the parish of Buckfastleigh (which includes Buckfast).

The Paper Mill, Buckfastleigh.

Situated on the banks of the River Dart, between Dartbridge and Austins Bridge, it is known to have been in existence from 1785–1942, when it was closed. Paper and woollen mills were often found together in the same area – both needing a good supply of clean water for power and the manufacturing process. Pasteboard made at the paper mill was needed for packing bales of serge (two pasteboards to every 'long ell') and the woollen mills supplied the felt needed for the paper making machinery.

Wheelwrights at Plymouth Road, Buckfastleigh *c*. 1900.

(Courtesy of Mrs K. Edworthy)

It was here that carts, wagons, gates and wheels for people of the surrounding district, including Buckfast, were made. The making of wheels is a highly skilled craft. William Hoare, who owned the business, can be seen second from the right, with his son Henry on the extreme left, and a Mr Hatch on the extreme right.

It is recorded that in 1588, five pairs of wheels were made at Buckfastleigh for the gun carriages to be used in the defence of Plymouth against the Spanish Armada. It is quite possible that these wheelwrights were descendants of those sixteenth century craftsmen – as Dom. John Stephan points out in his writings 'the names we meet on old documents, are still very common locally. Some have changed their addresses, but few have disappeared altogether. Four hundred years are bound to affect the fortunes of ordinary families, besides changes of occupation, unavoidable during such a long period – but the working man too, has his ancestry, even if it is not so copiously recorded as that of the more fortunate members of society'.

Bulley Cleaves limestone quarry *c*. 1929.

(Courtesy of Mr K. Fricker)

Bulley Cleaves, better known as Black Rock Quarry, was once owned by the Reverend Baring-Gould of Lewtrenchard. He was the Grandfather of the Rev. Sabine Baring-Gould, who wrote the famous hymn *Onward Christian Soldiers*. In 1839 he sold the quarry to William Coulton of Dean Prior, Buckfastleigh. In order to complete the purchase Coulton and his twelve-year-old grandson rode across Dartmoor to Lewtrenchard, the other side of Tavistock, with their saddlebags full of gold sovereigns. The journey there and back being completed the same day.

The quarry was owned by the Coulton family until 1928 when it was leased to Reginald Coles, of Cole Bros, Peasedown St John, Bath, who had obtained the contract to widen Dartbridge. The quarry, being nearby, was the obvious source of building material for this project. When the work was completed in 1929, Mr Coles formed his own company, known as R. W. Coles Quarries Ltd. Stone from the quarry was used to build and resurface most of the roads within a radius of about fifteen miles. Other important building works for which the limestone was used included the restoration of Buckfast

Bulley Cleaves limestone quarry *c.* 1929. *(Courtesy of Mr K. Fricker)*

Abbey, the construction of St Benedict's Catholic Church in Buckfastleigh and the sea-front at Torquay, from the pier to Torre Abbey sands. In 1961 the quarry was bought by the Bath and Portland Company who then traded as Kingston Minerals. It closed in 1975 because it was feared that the blasting would damage the foundations of the nearby parish church.

In this photo can be seen the workmen and their tools – a wheelbarrow, picks and shovels, and a small skip. This was probably part of the workforce that came to Buckfast with Cole Bros. Prior to their arrival, there was just one man working the quarry full time – William Hancock, who lived in the nearby Bulley Cleave Cottages. Everything was done manually – instead of pneumatic drills, there was just a 'jumper' (a heavy iron bar) and a sledgehammer. The 'jumper' was used to make a hole in the rock, and when deep enough it was packed with explosive, which was stored in Hancock's backyard. A long fuse was attached and when lit he would beat a hasty retreat to take cover. Once the blast had split the rock into large lumps, it would then be broken into smaller pieces with the sledgehammer. The

older residents of Buckfast can recall the rhythmic clanging of the 'jumper' as its sound echoed around the quarry.

Another important product of the quarry was lime, which was used for a great variety of purposes. This was produced by the burning of limestone at a very high temperature in limekilns. There were many such kilns in the area – all now redundant.

'Quick mother, 'ers got the gapes – fetch the lime'. This was said in jest by an old Devonshire man, when a visitor to his house started coughing and sneezing; What did he mean? Apparently, at one time, when chicken suffered from a complaint known as 'the gapes', the treatment was to put them in a box of lime, and shake it gently. The lime acted like snuff and caused the chicken to cough up the gapeworm which had lodged in its windpipe causing it to wheeze and 'gape'.

Though apples were plentiful in the area, there was one lorry driver from Broadhempston who did not follow the old adage 'An apple a day keeps the doctor away' – instead he had a knob of lime a day; dissolved in a glass of water.

Lime has been used for hundreds of years –

the Romans used it to make mortar – and farmers applied it to their land to reduce the acidity in the soil.

In a sixteenth century document relating to a plan of the parish church the quarry is mentioned thus: 'This ys the quarrye for the Kyngs tennts to bild there howsys and to marlee there grounde to bring forth corne'.

For centuries lime was believed to have antiseptic properties. In 1982 archaeologists, whilst excavating land under what is now the Abbey car park, discovered a large skeleton (over five feet long) of a hog. It had been buried in lime about 1800, probably because it had a disease such as swine fever.

Locally the principal uses of lime – in addition to agriculture – were, the processing of skins at the Buckfastleigh Tanyard, for limewashing sheds and cottages, and as the main ingredient in the making of 'lime ash' floors – when it was mixed with gravel and water to form a hard surface, though this was gradually superseded in the twentieth century by the introduction of cement.

Bulley Cleaves Quarry c. 1928. (*Courtesy of Mr K. Fricker*)
A hopper over which a rotary screen was placed sorted stones into various sizes, as required.

Bulley Cleaves Quarry *c.* 1938.
(Courtesy of Charles Coulton Stewart)

The solitary figure, centre left, is the general foreman Bert Brown. Bernard Parsons and Charlie Searle are standing by the skip. Bernard, who lived at nearby Faeries Hall, was noted for wearing a clean white shirt every day (ex Senior Service of course). One of the men loading the lorry would probably also be the driver – Arthur Nicholls. He and Charlie Searle came down from Bath, together with Percy Fricker, who supervised the installation of the machinery plant. It was to Mr Fricker that the building monks went when their saws and other tools needed sharpening.

The cottages seen behind the crusher, on the left, were Bulley Cleaves Cottages. Mr Hancock lived in one of them with his wife and family. Until recently they were used as offices, by A.R.C. Ltd (Associated Roadstone Corporation Ltd). The building in the centre background is Blackrock House, currently a hotel.

The tarmac plant at Bulley Cleaves Quarry *c.* 1946. *(Courtesy of Mr K. Fricker)*

The dust raised from the quarry used to settle on the nearby cottages and Blackrock House, and on everything and everybody within the vicinity. Dust suppressors were later developed and fitted to the plant.

Inevitably, over the years, there were serious accidents from time to time with at least two fatalities – Bill Dunn and Alvin Wills.

Local Saying: 'You'd best go down Bulley Cleaves and carve 'eself one' – said to anyone being over-critical.

Buckfast Gas Works *c.* 1950. *(Courtesy of Mr B. Milsom British Gas Plc, Keynsham)*

The first gasworks in Buckfast was built in 1868, but details of those early days are not well documented. The builder was a George Bower of St Neots, Huntingdonshire.

An entrepreneur, Frederick Pope of Britton Peverill House, near Bath, set out in 1890 to purchase undertakings, mainly gas and waterworks, selling them at a handsome profit to limited companies which he himself had formed. He purchased the works at Buckfast for £3000 and in June 1893 a new company was formed with a capital of £5000 to purchase from him. It appears that raising the capital was not easy and his creditors obtained judgement against him and this venture failed. Following this it would seem that the Buckfastleigh Gas Company was formed in 1898. At the turn of the century, attempts were made to protect small, vulnerable non-statutory gas works by bringing them into groups. In 1906, the Devon Gas Association Ltd was registered with a capital of £6000 in £10 shares. Buckfastleigh was transferred to this Association on 5 October, 1912.

By 1931 the Devon Gas Association had eleven works and eight of these were in competition with the electricity undertakings. It is interesting to note that Buckfastleigh Urban District Council switched back to gas public lighting for an initial period of seven years after using electricity for the previous twenty. The price of gas produced at Buckfast had been deliberately reduced to achieve this.

Ashburton Urban District Council sold their gas undertaking to the Association, and after

extensions to the Buckfast works, a five-inch main was laid between the two at a cost of £2000 and the Ashburton works closed, Buckfast thus becoming the sole supplier.

In 1949 the entire industry was nationalised and run by area boards. The South Western Gas Board extended the main from Totnes to Buckfast, and from then on both Buckfastleigh and Ashburton were supplied with gas manufactured at the works in Torquay and stored in the Buckfast gasometer. Buckfast production ceased in 1950. The gasometer was used for storage until 1985 when it was demolished.

During the General Strike of 1926, coal supplies were not getting through to Buckfastleigh railway station and stocks were running low. The late Richard Dinwiddy, station master, recalled that the gasworks

manager, Joe Maddocks, bought nearly 200 tons of pit props that had been stockpiled at the station yard at the end of the Great War. By careful mixing of coal and wood the gasworks continued its supply, though no mention is made of its quality!

Throughout its long life the gasworks played an important part in the life of the village. Coke was sold 'by the bag' and locals used to fill the largest sack they could find, the price (a few pence) was the same whatever the size. Tar was another by-product, used as a wood preservative, and generous measures were the order of the day. The last manager of the gas-works was Horace Stephens.

The coaches seen in the photograph stand in the Buckfastleigh Urban Council car park, where now stands the new mill extension.

The Manager Joe Maddocks standing on the foundation of a new gasometer *c.* 1930.
(*Courtesy of Mr B. Maddocks*)

On a Sunday morning, when most households were cooking the Sunday lunch, the gas pressure would sometimes drop. Housewives would ring up, or visit the plant, to complain and on most occasions the pressure was increased.

The retort house was a favourite stopover in cold, wet weather for many tramps, or 'milestone inspectors' as they were known by the villagers. They used to 'invade' the village for a free meal (three courses and coffee) provided by the Abbey. It has been said that as many as forty tramps had been counted in a day. The local police became concerned and the Abbey authorities were advised to reduce their hospitality in order to discourage so many visitors, some of whom were involved in petty theft. Sandwiches eventually replaced the cooked meals and the numbers gradually reduced.

Other regular visitors to the retort house were he local lads of the football team. After each match they took a free hot bath and emerged clean and scrubbed, ready for a Saturday night out. Local girls were often seen in the vicinity of the gas works on a Saturday evening!

During the last war local ARP wardens used the stoke house to warm themselves on cold winter nights.

FISHING

Today salmon fishing is looked upon as a sport and relaxation, but to the Cistercian monks, in pre-Reformation days, fish from the River Dart was an important source of food.

From very early times, there has been legislation regarding the 'free passage' of fish in the river. Prior to 1539, there were several disputes between the monks of Buckfast and their neighbours. The most notable being one which took place in the late fourteenth century when the Abbot of Buckfast, a Robert Simons, led a band of inhabitants to Staverton, about four miles downstream to investigate why no fish were coming up. They realised that the river must have been blocked in some way. The Abbot literally took the law into his own hands and, together with his band of men, destroyed the weirs there, ransacked the mills, cut up the nets and generally created havoc. Though this scene of destruction led to the Abbot having to pay a fine, his fishing rights were never again questioned. A strange sequel to this story is that only a few years later, the Staverton stretch of fishing was made over to the Abbot of Buckfast in 1395 and it remained Abbey property until the Dissolution in 1539.

Fishing at Buckfastleigh – a print published in 1829.

This scene would be familiar to those who fish the river Dart today, in fact just over a hundred years after this print was published,

a record-breaking salmon was caught in almost the same spot by Donald Beard (the author's father). It weighed 33lbs and was caught on the 11 May, 1930. This still stands as a record for a salmon caught by rod and line – although there have been larger fish caught by net in the lower reaches of the Dart.

The print was published fifty-three years before the return of the Benedictine monks to Buckfast. The present Abbey would be situated to the right of the mansion house. The ruins of the fifteenth century Abbot's Tower can just be seen behind the hay wain.

Donald Beard fishing at Buckfast Weir *c.* 1930.

Salmon fishing, as a sport, had its hey-day at Buckfast in the first half of the twentieth century. People came from far and wide in order to fish this beautiful stretch of the River Dart. Amongst those who came regularly was the cartoonist George Studdy, famous for his 'Bonzo' dog character.

Donald Beard with his record-breaking salmon 11 May 1930.

An original autograph by George Studdy, drawn for the author's Mother whilst staying at Northwood, Buckfast, in 1932.

Other well known personalities who came to Northwood to fish were the Hardy brothers. Their company 'The House of Hardy' still manufactures world famous fishing tackle, regarded by many as the Rolls-Royce of the sport.

John James Hardy fishing a pool just below Buckfast Abbey *c.* 1920.

One of five brothers, J. J. Hardy, was the Professional Champion Salmon and Trout Flycaster of Europe and the author of several specialist books on fly fishing and fly dressing. He died in 1932.

The late Lady Rose Bowes-Lyon, a sister of Her Majesty the Queen Mother, was also a visitor, as were the Crawfords (of biscuit fame) and the Wolseleys (of motor-car fame).

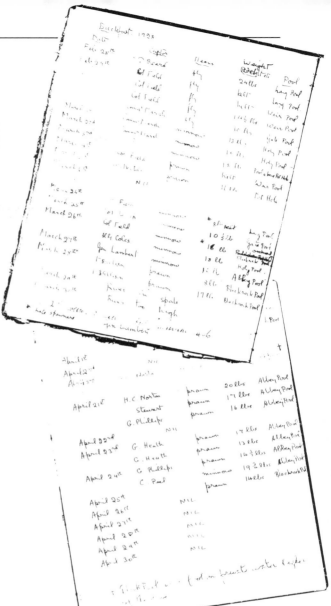

This bungalow was specially built at Northwood Farm to accommodate the fishing visitors.

A fisherman's log book for March and April, 1928. *(Courtesy of Mr H. G. Coles)*

In 1933, the Dart Fishery Board described the middle reaches of the river (which includes the Buckfast stretch) as 'very good spring salmon water'. A total of twenty-nine salmon (though four were kelts – fish that had spawned) were caught during this period, and the baits used were: fly, minnow, and prawn.

The water bailiff, Fred Mugford (second from left) *c.* 1935.

Fred Mugford was well known as the water bailiff for many years, he was the friend of all the fishermen and the formidable enemy of the poacher. Some locals still remember him today with affection, though as children when 'fishing' for eels on a bent pin, they remember the call 'look out Fred is coming, tell him we *are* using bent pins' (not hooks). During the spawning season he used to stay on Dartmoor to guard the fish on their spawning grounds, armed with a 12-bore shotgun.

The gentleman on the left is John Fogden – the other two are not known. The group are netting salmon during a period of low water, and transferring them to deeper water above the weir from where they can continue their journey upstream.

Jack Burt and Eric Woodward *c.* 1950.
(Courtesy of Mrs R. Walters)
Mr Woodward and members of his family have fished the river between Dartbridge and Hembury Woods for over ninety years.

Preparing to pack a fish to send home *c*. 1948.
(Courtesy of Mrs D. Kent)
Eric Woodward watching Bill Kent preparing
a salmon frail, or rush basket, in readiness to
send his catch home. This scene was taken
in the 'fishermans hut' at Furzeleigh Mill
Guest House.

**Raymond Foale, the huntsman of the
Dartmoor Otter Hounds at work** *c*. 1938.
In order to protect the fishing, the local
landowners, and the water bailiff in
particular, encouraged the hunting of otters.

Since 1978 the otter has been a protected
animal. There have been few recorded
sightings on the river since about
1960 – though their decline has not been
directly attributed to hunting, which ceased at
the beginning of the last war. Wild mink are
probably the main culprits.

THE ONES THAT DIDN'T GET AWAY

A visitor to Northwood, Capt F. B. Ellison with two salmon (8 and 17lb) caught at Blackrock. *(Courtesy of Mr H. G. Coles)*

A successful catch *c.* 1920 – Edward Bovey with the Nortons, father and son. *(Courtesy of Mrs Walters)*

Harold Coles at Northwood with an 18lb salmon. *(Courtesy of Mr H. G. Coles)*

John Beard (right) with Mr Bryant and a large sea trout.

Right: Fishing Monks.
Below: Arthur Burgess, a visitor to North-wood, contributed this entry to the autograph book of the author's grandmother, 1918.

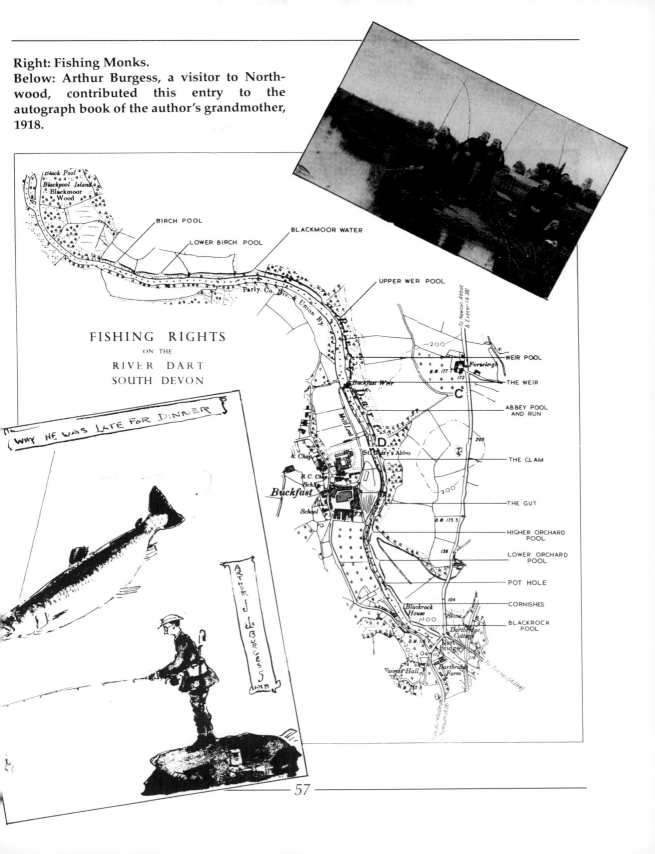

FISHING RIGHTS
ON THE
RIVER DART
SOUTH DEVON

Black Pool
Blackpool Island
Blackmoor Wood

BIRCH POOL

LOWER BIRCH POOL

BLACKMOOR WATER

UPPER WER POOL

WEIR POOL

THE WEIR

ABBEY POOL AND RUN

THE CLAM

THE GUT

HIGHER ORCHARD POOL

LOWER ORCHARD POOL

POT HOLE

CORNISHES

BLACKROCK POOL

WHY HE WAS LATE FOR DINNER

ARTHUR J BURGESS 1918

SCHOOLS

In common with many Devon villages, little attention was paid to the formal education of children until the latter years of the nineteenth century. The early schools did little more than teach the rudiments of reading, writing and arithmetic, and attendance at school always came second to seasonal farmwork.

Buckfast Abbey Church site, 1906.
The small rectangular building on the right was a school known as the Alumnate. This was the monastic school for boys showing a religious vocation. Between 1884 and 1917, some 132 pupils passed through the school and 75 became monks or priests. These boys, some of them as young as ten, generally followed the same timetable as the monks, except they did not get up at 2am for Matins. They rose at 5.15am all the year round. The Alumnate was built by Bishop Vaughan of Plymouth and was eventually demolished to make way for the building of the west front of the new Abbey Church.

Some Alumnii (pupils) 10 August, 1910.
(Courtesy of Buckfast Abbey)

The monk second left standing at the back is
Dom John Stephan, then about twenty-six
years of age and probably a teacher at the
Alumnate. He was later to become a Fellow of
the Royal Historical Society and wrote a
history of Buckfast Abbey. Brother Ignatius
Birk, fourth left at the back became one of the
principal builders of the new Abbey Church.
Sitting in the front row (extreme left) is Martin
Henle who later left and farmed at Dartbridge.
His brother became a priest, Father William
Henle, who was Prior of Buckfast Abbey from
1931 to 1937. Brother Adam Kehrle is seated
second right. He had then only just arrived
aged twelve, and had not yet received his
habit! As most will already know, he is now a
world authority on the breeding of bees and
bee-keeping, and has received several
international awards, and the OBE, for his
contribution to apiculture.

St Mary's Convent School *c.* 1901.
(Courtesy of Mr R. Crook)

This was a Roman Catholic school, built in 1893. The first nuns came in 1901. They were the 'Sisters of Charity', famous for their huge white coifs, known affectionately by some as 'God's Geese'. At the time of its opening the school had 160 pupils taught by lay teachers. Though it was a Catholic school, any denomination was accepted. Now it is a Primary School only – though up until the late fifties children were educated until school leaving age.

In 1914 a different order of nuns took over the teaching – the Sisters of the Holy Ghost, who had a fee paying convent school at Ingsdon, near Newton Abbot. They remained until 1927 when Sister Laurence Ryan and other nuns of the Congregation of Charity of St Paul, from Birmingham, took over the running of the school. Sister Laurence ruled it with a rod of iron (or was it a cane?) for thirty-three years. Though she was strict, she is remembered by many with affection. She had to be strict, there were no male teachers and it was a mixed school. The Convent, with its teaching nuns, closed at the beginning of 1987 – but the school is still a Roman Catholic primary.

Schoolchildren dance around the maypole at Kennel Field, Northwood
c. 1904.

SCHOLARS		
1. Maud CROOK	16. Rev. Mother Sister MARY	31. Bessie BAKER
2. Colin PAUL	17. Lilian BEARD	32. Tom McCARTHY
3. Beatrice CROOK	18. Sister JOSEPH	33. Emma FOSTER
4. Wilfred FORD	19. Rose PARSONS	34. Ernest CROOK
5. Florrie NARRAMORE	20. Eva BOWMAN	35. Margot BEARD
6. Jack PROWSE	21. Jim BURT	36. Bert BAKER
7. May BEARD	22. Wilfred PARSONS	37. Amy BOWMAN
8. Bill NARRAMORE	23. Charlie HARDEN	38. Eva BOWMAN
9. John BURT	24. Nellie FOSTER (PROWSE)	39. Harry BAKER
10. Violet BEARD	25. Gertie FOSTER (PROWSE)	40. Arthur BAKER
11. Bill FOSTER	26. George McCARTHY	41. Olive KING
12. Father MELLITUS HAULER	27. Nellie PARSONS	42. Leonard PROWSE
13. Martha NARRAMORE	28. Bill McCARTHY	43. Nellie McCARTHY
14. Sister VINCENT	29. Gladdie PROWSE	44. Dorothy BEARD
15. Maud BAKER	30. Hubert FORD	45. Bernard PARSONS

Buckfast Church of England School, 1915.
(Courtesy of Miss W. Coram)
Though the monks of Buckfast received much support from the local community in the early days, there was still an 'anti-Catholic' feeling amongst some. The local people therefore decided to build their own school so that their children would not have to attend the 'Papist School'. It was completed in 1894 just a year after the Convent School. The average attendance was always lower than the 'other school' and in 1920 it was decided to close it.

The pupils shown here are:

Back row left to right.
Ralph Hancock, Gwen Searle, Violet Wood, Kathleen Wood, Lilian Routley and Ernie Coram.
Next row.
Miss Lee, Bill Thorne, Bill Hopkins, Avis Hancock, Jimmy Gruit, Winston Routley and Miss Gillard.

Next row.
Mildred Parsons, Jane Northcott, Horace Wood, Bert Wood, Arthur Dawe, Lily Hopkins, Flora Carro, Charlie Coram and Leslie Coram.
Front row.
Dorothy Lody, Wilfred Northcott, Lloyd Routley, Howell Hughes, Eva Northcott, Isabel Searle, Elsie Wood, Winnie Coram, Ada Wood and Gilbert Hancock.

One boy who attended this school was Cecil Wood. Born in 1900 he was a pupil from 1903 until 1911 when the local doctors became concerned about his health. They told his parents not to send him to school any more, but to let him 'run free'.

Though not a Catholic, he spent most of his time with Brother Emmanuel Dillenz who used to drive the Abbey horse and cart. Much of their time was spent carting Bath stone from Buckfastleigh railway station, and limestone from the local quarries. Sometimes they went to Dundridge, near Totnes, the home of Sir Robert Harvey (it was Sir Robert who donated the bells to the Abbey in memory of his late wife). The visit to Dundridge was to collect empty wine bottles which the Abbey then used to bottle their own tonic wine. On the 15 April, 1912 whilst on such a trip, word came through that the *Titanic* had sunk. When they returned in the evening (the trip took all day) Cecil told his parents and neighbours the news, but they ridiculed him and said it could not happen. Of course, the next day the disaster was reported in all the newspapers.

The older inhabitants of Buckfast spoke of Brother Emmanuel with great respect, and Cecil Wood referred to him as 'a perfect gentleman'.

Despite Cecil's education finishing at the age of eleven, he went on to become the manager of a large grocery department at the Totnes Co-operative Wholesale Society, and was also responsible for the accounts of the bakery, butchery and dairy departments of the same store.

At the risk of embarrassing Cecil, I would describe him in the same way as he described Brother Emmanuel 'a perfect gentleman'. When last seen at the age of ninety-one, he was a smart, upright gentleman and was most diplomatic and discreet when talking about people and events. He would never speak ill of anyone.

Contemporary view of Buckfast Church of England School – now known as the Violet Evelyn Institute.

In 1920 a Mr Fleming bought the school and gave it to the village in memory of his daughter Violet Evelyn. It was used as a church/sunday school for the Church of England community in the village. With the decline in attendances at the once a month service, the building was acquired, ironically, by the Abbey. The last service was held on the 7 January, 1990.

FARMING

The richer soils of the moorland fringe and the lush pasturelands bordering the River Dart encouraged farming from the earliest times at Buckfast. No doubt the original religious community here established a strong agricultural tradition to provide for its own needs.

The land around Buckfast reflects the pattern of centuries of farming, with neat, irregular fields surrounding stone and slate farmsteads. Only since the war has agriculture given way as the major occupation in the region and the photographs that follow recall those more tranquil days.

Molly and Madam pulling the binder at Northwood Farm *c.* 1938.

Top: **Harvesting the rabbits** *c.* 1938.
Bottom: **The author and her brother** *c.* 1940.

A threshing scene at Northwood Farm *c*. 1938.

The threshing machine and steam engine travelled from farm to farm in the area. Neighbouring farmers helped each other as it needed at least ten people to keep the operation going. One of the travelling threshing men used to chew tobacco – he was said to have a deadly aim.

Three neighbouring farmers *c*. 1928.
Father Winfrid Rechtsteiner of the Abbey Farm, Donald Beard of Northwood Farm, and Martin Henle of Dartbridge Farm. Father Winfrid was a priest of many talents. Not only was he a knowledgeable farmer, but at times was the organist, parish priest, procurator, and worked in the pharmacy and the tonic wine department. The Poo Bah of the Monastery!

Monks ploughing and planting potatoes on their farmland *c*. 1940.
(Courtesy of Buckfast Abbey)

'Salmon Leap' cafe and guest house.

The Grange *c*. 1943.

Inset: Gilbert Scott with Bessie and haysweep at the Grange *c*. 1920.
Grange House can just be seen to the left, and the roof of the ancient tithe barn in the background.

Both the buildings in these photographs were destroyed by fire and no longer exist. Grange House was burnt down and eventually demolished in 1986. There is now a private housing estate on the site and adjoining farmland.

The original Grange (meaning 'farm') and tithe barn was the main 'home farm' for the medieval monastery at Buckfast. The tithe barn, built in the thirteenth or fourteenth century, would have been used to store produce, wool and grain. Parts of the structure survive, though it has been converted to dwellings.

The 'Salmon Leap' cafe and guest house, stood on the site of the present day 'Little Chef' restaurant at Dart Bridge. It was burnt down and demolished in 1975.

TRANSPORT

Before the Dissolution of the Monasteries the monks themselves were responsible for upkeep of the roads and for bridge building. For carriage of goods and produce the packhorse was the favoured mode of transportation in Devon until better roads allowed the use of horse-drawn wagons and, later, steam wagons. Today traffic rushes past on the nearby busy A38, close to Dartbridge where once the London mail coach made its painful way to and from the capital. In 1872 the railway arrived at Buckfastleigh bringing more prosperity to the area. Part of the line still survives today between Buckfastleigh and Staverton and is known as The South Devon Railway 'Primrose Line' run by a charitable trust.

Outside Buckfast Abbey Mansion House *c. 1910. (Courtesy of Mr R. Crook)*
George Cove (at the pony's head) and Bill Mugford. The steps in the background lead up to the house, which was built in 1806 with stones from the ruins of the medieval Abbey. The present monastery building incorporates this house (and the steps now lead up to the

reception rooms). In front of the steps is now the porch and door leading to the monastery, with the visitors parlours on either side of the steps. Mr Cove was a gardener at the Abbey most of his life, Mr Mugford worked in the nearby woollen mill.

Traffic accident at Dartbridge *c.* 1920.
(Courtesy Mr K Fricker)
Prior to the 1930s, steam wagons were the main force of heavy transport. This one was carrying a load of stone – perhaps for road mending? Part of the Toll House can be seen on the extreme right and Furzeleigh Mill (then a corn mill) can just be seen to the left of the engine funnel. The roads were unmetalled, most of them being resurfaced with tarmac in the mid twenties.

An old Buckfast saying (often said to a worrier): 'You'm gwain Dart bridge to meet it', meaning 'you're looking for trouble'.

Buckfast Mother's Union outing, 1928.
(Courtesy Miss W. Coram)

Some stalwarts of the parish setting out on one of their annual charabanc outings.

Back row from left to right.
Polly Searle, Louise Roberts, Miss Annie Lewis (nicknamed 'The Duchess' by some!) and Mrs Hancock holding Dorothy Hancock.

Next row.
Edie Cove, Ethel Cottle, Florence Northcott, and Mary Jane Widdecombe (standing).

Next row.
Elizabeth Searle holding Hette Searle, Alice Maddocks, Bessie King and Lizzie Burt (standing).

Front row.
Bessie Coram, the driver (believed to be Ted Tucker), an unknown lady and Jane Ash (standing).

The charabanc belongs to J. Millman & Sons, a family coach firm still in existence.

A war-time ambulance *c.* 1943.
Mildred Beard of Buckfast beside her vehicle –

ready for an emergency call. Note the 'blackout' headlamps – three tiny slits of light. Being a newly-qualified driver, an emergency call after dark must have been particularly hair-raising, both to driver and patients. Mrs B. recalls one such occasion transporting three soldiers injured whilst training on Scorriton Down, to Newton Abbot Hospital. The entrance to the hospital is on a steep slope, and on arrival the gates were closed. She discovered to her horror that the handbrake would not hold and one of the injured patients had to scramble out to let them in. Whether he and his colleagues lived to tell the tale is not known!

Looping the loop at Paignton, 1930
Mrs Mildred Beard of Buckfast, on the extreme left, just before the aircraft took off from the Green, alongside Paignton beach, for a short flight over Torbay. During the flight they looped the loop, for which dubious pleasure the passengers had to pay more. They were not strapped in.

Buckfastleigh Railway Station *c.* 1905.
At this time, being part of the Great Western
Railway, it was a very busy branch line.
Freight carried included wool for the mills,
skins for the tanyard in Buckfastleigh, coal,
cider etc., as well as truck loads of cattle on
Ashburton market days, and race horses and
their grooms when Buckfastleigh races took
place.

The passenger train known by everyone as
'Bulliver' is still remembered by school
children who attended their respective
grammar schools at Ashburton and Totnes.

Pupils can still recall that during the Second
World War there were occasions when they
had to travel by bus, or were delayed. This
caused much excitement, because although
the reason was supposed to be 'top secret'
they knew that the Royal Train had been
'stabled' overnight in a siding near Staverton,
when their Majesties were visiting the West
Country. To the security services, including
the railway staff this operation was known as
'Deep Dene'.

Passenger trains ceased in 1958 and goods
trains in 1962.

Logos of the SDR 'Primrose Line'.

PEOPLE OF BUCKFAST

The faces and characters shown in the following photographs are part of the more recent history of the ancient village of Buckfast. However some of the local family names can be traced back for centuries.

Felling trees near Dartbridge *c.* 1910.
(*Courtesy of the late Mr R. Lewis*)
From left to right: Sidney Lewis, Jack Burt and Dick Lewis. Dick Lewis was the village handyman to whom the villagers turned whether it be to kill a pig, fell a tree or build a wall.

An example of Dick Lewis's handiwork.
These piers which he and some monks constructed in 1917, were used, when spanned by planks, to transport sand from the River Dart bank opposite to the Abbey where it was used in the building of the Abbey Church. This is the site of an ancient ford which led to the market town of Ashburton, hence the name Priestaford for the large house nearby.

Hosking & Sons – Builders and carpenters for over fifty years.
Fernley Hosking and his younger brother Ashton, with their father Richard Sydney Hosking on their Royal Enfield motorbike and sidecar. This photograph was taken at the rear of 5 Plymouth Road, Buckfastleigh *c.* 1913.

Ashton Hosking (centre), together with his father and their apprentice, Fred Northcote, made all the oak doors of the Church at Buckfast Abbey. They also built several houses and bungalows in the village of Buckfast, including Sideham, Winsley, Shyrehill and Hockmoor. Ashton Hosking was also responsible, in 1939, for building the Catholic Church in Buckfastleigh.

Extract from the Monastic 'Chimes' *c.* 1922.

Chimes Echoes

The gigantic doors, which form a great feature of this West Front, were fixed on their massive hinges in time for the feast of All Saints. It is interesting to record that such a piece of joinery could be undertaken by a local youth, Mr. Ashton Hosking, of Buckfastleigh. Together with his father, this young man is responsible for most of the beautiful oak-doors in the Abbey church. It is not many carpenters who are called upon to produce doors weighing half-a-ton, and we are really happy to give young Hosking the credit he deserves for having inspired the confidence of our architect, and given proofs of such efficiency in his craft. The hinges, designed by Mr. F. A. Walters, have been wrought by Messrs. Reynolds & Co., London. These doors are a picture in themselves.

A group of school children from Buckfast 1 August, 1935.
Taken on board the SS *President Roosevelt* as the children were setting off on a trip to France. The ship was used as a troop carrier during the Second World War, when it was renamed USS *Joseph T. Dickman*. This ship rescued the crew of a British cargo ship *Antinoe* during a mid-Atlantic gale in 1926.

Left to right.

Standing: P. Cousins, F. Witt, M. Ash, P. Clark, Miss C. Hodgson, M. Clark and D. Fricker. *Seated:* M. Tape, Father John Stephan (the Parish Priest), Miss Maddicott, and Capt. Barry.

Front row.
M. Sampson, P. Northcott, H. Searle, J. Burge, D. Grute, H. Fricker and V. Tapper.

**The Parish Priest – Father Mellitus Hauler –
with the Buckfast School Guides and Scouts**
c. 1931. (*Courtesy of the late Mr R. Lewis*)

Left to right.
Back row: Jimmy Lear, Edwin Lear, Colin Ford,
Annie Lewis, Rene Turvy, Betty Tapper, Jimmy
Flood, William Ash, and George Freeman.
Middle row: Ethel Turner, Ruth Searle, Father
Mellitus Hauler (then Parish Priest), Ivy Abbot
and Maud Cottle. *Front row:* Maurice Turner
(killed in 1939/45 war), Jimmy Burge, Dido
Lewis and Freddie Witt.

Washing day at Buckfast *c.* 1930. (*Courtesy of
the late Mr L. Coram*)

Left to right.
Miss Violet Ash (later Mrs Lewis) with flasket,
Mrs Jane Ash and Mrs Bessie Coram, with their
washing in front of New Buildings. The present
Buckfast Nursery is on the site of the then allot-
ments, and the washing lines were to the side
of them, adjacent to the public footpath known
as Pathfields.

William Ash on the occasion of his eightieth birthday, 1956.

He is standing with the then Abbot of Buckfast, the Right Rev. Dom Placid Hooper. Mr Ash was a Verger at Buckfast for many years, both in the temporary church and the new Abbey Church. He used to enjoy telling the tale of how he failed to recognise the Duke of Norfolk, Earl Marshall of England and the leading Roman Catholic layman in the country. Apparently there was a special service in the temporary church. Just as the service began, Mr Ash who was at the back of the church, felt someone pluck his sleeve and say 'Shouldn't I have a better place than this?' Mr Ash replied 'Who are you Sir?'. 'I'm the Duke of Norfolk'. Whereupon Mr Ash beckoned to Abbot Vonier who came down from his place in the choir stalls to greet the Duke, and escort him to his reserved seat.

Presentation of Royal Humane Society's Certificate to an Alumnus from the Abbey *c.* 1914. *(Courtesy of Mrs W. Penwill)*

One summer the monks were swimming in the River Dart, when Father Ernest got into difficulties and nearly drowned. He was rescued by Brother Hugh, who was then only a young Alumnus being educated by the community. In the picture Father Bernard Vaughan, a well known Jesuit Priest and orator, is seen presenting the certificate to Brother Hugh. Father Ernest is facing the camera, while Abbot Vonier looks on. On the extreme right are Father John Stephan and Father Winfrid Rechtsteiner. Father Dominic (then Brother Henry) was also involved in the rescue and he received a medal for his efforts.

The Beard Family at Northwood, *c.* 1904.

A group of monks taking a rest during their afternoon walk *c. 1939. (Courtesy of Miss M. Farrell)*

At one time it was a familiar sight to see groups of monks taking a walk in the country lanes that surround Buckfast Abbey. The practice declined in the sixties and seventies probably due to the increasing age of the existing monks, and the lack of new entrants to the novitiate.

Left to right.

Brothers Paul, Matthias, Hilarion, Vincent, Paschal, Bernard and Columban (who used to look after the bees before Brother Adam, and was well known for his 'honey cake' which he used to make in the Abbey kitchens).

The Bourbon Bell, 1936.

This huge $7\frac{1}{2}$ ton bell was presented to the Abbey by Miss Hilda de Trafford in memory of her sister, Lady Bellew. It was hoisted into the belfry in 1936. In this picture left to right: Miss de Trafford, Father Adalbert Pappelau, Father Erconwald Plersh, Father Winfrid Rechsteiner, Abbot Vonier and Father Stephen Kramer (a parish priest of Ashburton for many years). Father Adalbert Pappelau will be remembered by many for he was in charge of, and served in the Abbey religious shops for over fifty years – retiring in his eighties. He was also captain of the bellringers for many years and during the last war was an A.R.P. (Air Raid Precautions) Warden. The names of the two workmen up the ladder are not known.

Abbot Vonier and monks walking the dog *c. 1930.*

Wedding group Whit Monday 17 June, 1917.

Two farming families were united when Hedley Sampson of Bowerdon Farm and Violet Beard of Northwood Farm were married.

1. Reg SAMPSON
2. Gilbert SCOTT
3. Edith SCOTT
4. George INCLEDON
5. Donald BEARD
6. Miss BAKER (of the Buckfast Post Office)
7. Dick WILLCOCKS
8. Mrs Will SAMPSON – 'Minne'
9. Ernie SAMPSON
10. ?
11. Mrs MATTY – 'Ginny' (nee Lewis)
12. ?

13. Mrs Emma SCOTT (nee Lewis)
14. Mrs Winnie ABBOT
15. Miss Annie LEWIS
16. Mr MATTY
17. Henry BEARD
18. Capt. BERRINGTON
19. Mrs BERRINGTON
20. May BEARD
21. Henry SAMPSON
22. Emily SAMPSON
23. Hedley SAMPSON (the Groom)
24. Violet BEARD (the Bride)

25. John BEARD
26. Elizabeth BEARD
27. Nellie BEARD
28. Mr SCOTT (from Fernworthy near Chagford)
29. Polly HEWITT (nee Scott)
30. Edith WARREN (later Walters)
31. Will SAMPSON
32. Lilian BEARD (later Henle)
33. Margot BEARD (later Cousins)
34. Hetty SAMPSON (later Goodman)
35. Gwen HEWITT (later Heesom)

36. John SCOTT
37. Rita BEARD
38. Dorothy BEARD
39. Henry SAMPSON
40. Mrs William BEARD
41. Horace SAMPSON

Old Buckfast saying: 'You'm overhatted like the Totnes man'. The origin of this is unknown.

BUCKFAST
THEN AND NOW

The following pictures have been selected to reflect on the rapidity with which changes have been wrought upon the village, not only by the growth of the Abbey and the Mill, but by the development of the road system.

Buckfast Village *c.* 1890.
(Courtesy of Mr R. Crook)
This view would have been a familiar sight to the monks who arrived at Buckfast in 1882. It is taken from 'Shute Corner' and shows the thatched roofs of Northgate Cottages, thought to have been built in 1749 and demolished in the fifties and replaced with modern houses. Northgate Arch is hidden by the trees to the left, and the pointed spire of Buckfastleigh Parish Church can just be seen in the distance.

Shute Corner takes its name from a water shute that ran near the junction of Northwood Lane and Grange Road. The iron gratings can still be seen in the road there although the shute was blocked off in the early 1960s.

Northgate Arch *c.* 1910.

William Ash lived with his family in the little cottage on the right which was a small shop selling sweets and tobacco. The arch is mid twelfth century, and King Edward I passed under it in April 1297.

Contemporary view of Northgate Arch.

This ancient arch now has four concrete bollards directly underneath it, placed there in 1983 when the road was closed to through traffic.

Another view of Northgate Arch *c.* 1890.

Bee boles in old wall (1985).
These recesses in the wall were used to hold the traditional straw bee skips, showing that long before Brother Adam there were bees at Buckfast. These remains have now sadly fallen into disrepair.

Contemporary view of the Methodist Chapel.
Built in 1891 – one year before the monks returned to Buckfast – it is believed to have been constructed by members of the circuit. It is the last remaining building not belonging to the Abbey inside the ancient precinct.

Abbey Farm *c.* 1980.
A late fourteenth or early fifteenth century building, originally part of the huge Guest Hall complex belonging to the Abbey. In the nineteenth and early twentieth century it was used as a farmhouse by the Lewis family, and more recently as a restaurant and tea-room when this photo was taken. At the time of writing it is being restored.

At the beginning of this century it was tenanted by Miss Annie Lewis, who kept some cows, selling milk and cream to the villagers. Village gossip maintained that she kept an 'iron cow' in her garden. This was her water pump!

Door to the nineteenth century cider house.
This is sited at one end of the former Guest Hall.

Southgate Cottages *c.* 1930.
(*Courtesy of Miss W. Coram*)

Between the Convent on the left and the Working Men's Institute on the right, these cottages were demolished in the fifties. The junction of the new road takes their place on this site.

Another view of Southgate Cottages *c*. 1912.
(*Courtesy of Mr R. Crook*)

Also in the picture are the Working Men's Institute and the Barracks, with Berry's Mill behind the wall on the right. A Simon Berry, of the mill-owning family, had the Institute built for the men of Buckfast to provide a permanent centre for their leisure activities – concerts, billiards, etc. and prior to 1920 part of it was used as a Sunday School. It is believed to have been built in the late nineteenth century.

The building known as the Barracks is in the background. Recent archaeological excava-

Duncan Matheson and his mother in the garden of their house 'Rack Meadow', now 'Dovecote'. Northgate Cottages, thatched roof in background, but no Abbey tower!
c. 1908.

tions have revealed evidence of twelfth century foundations. This probably would of been part of the Cistercian Abbey precinct, hence the Southgate Arch. It is probable that John Berry, the mill owner then, built up on the ruins to form dwellings for his workers. One definition of 'Barracks' is 'a large plain building to house *en masse*'. Prior to 1967 parts of the building were used by the adjacent mill: the top floor as a store, and the 'room' over the arch had four blanket looms. The sound of these machines could be heard overhead when walking beneath the archway. To the left of the arch was the village shop known as 'Bezzells', Mr and Mrs Bezzell being the owners. Though smoking was strictly forbidden in the mill, it was not unknown for the workers at the looms to attract the attention of a passer by, throw them some money (2d) and persuade them to purchase a packet of five Woodbines, which would then be tied to a piece of string and carefully pulled back through the weaving shed window. From 1967 to 1983 the building housed a beautiful collection of shells, and now it belongs to the Abbey again, who plan to use it as residential quarters for their guests.

Contemporary scene of Southgate without the cottages.

Mrs Heather Chivall at the doorway at Northgate Cottages *c.* 1935, demolished in the fifties

The Toll House, Dartbridge.
(Courtesy of Mr K. Fricker)

Contemporary scene – following the demolition of the Toll House.

At one time the road here was a turnpike, the Toll House keeper collecting tolls for the upkeep of the road. Near here in July 1618 (on the road to Ashburton) Sir Walter Raleigh was arrested and taken to the Tower of London where he was later beheaded. The Toll House was demolished in the early seventies to make way for the new A38 road complex.

Buckfast Mill and cottages *c.* 1910.
Known as 'New Buildings' – there were two more rows of cottages behind these. The cottages facing the road were occupied by the foremen of the mill and had 'front parlours', which the others did not. In June 1950 these properties were bought and presented to the Buckfastleigh Urban District Council, together with money for repair and upkeep, by Miss Sylvia Calmady Hamlyn – 'to provide security for the tenants'. They were demolished in 1984 and a carpet showroom now stands on the site.

Contemporary scene – following the demolition of the cottages.

Aerial view of Buckfast *c.* 1934. (*Courtesy of Buckfast Abbey*)
Compare with the following photograph.

Aerial view of Buckfast, 1989.

Aerial view of Buckfast from the south-west, 1988. (*Courtesy of Buckfast Spinning Co. Ltd*)

The last year in which the car and caravan park were in use.

North wall of the south wing of the medieval guest hall during restoration, August 1991.

A crane lifts a four tonne roof truss into place, September 1991.

The Mill Shop, Buckfast Spinning Company, 1991.

The new mill extension, built 1989.

The Repository, Buckfast Abbey, for many years known as the Abbey tea rooms, demolished 1990.

The new Grange Restaurant and tea rooms on the site of the repository, opened August 1991.

Aerial view of Buckfast from the south-west, 1989. (*Courtesy of Buckfast Spinning Co. Ltd*) This clearly shows the extension to Buckfast Spinning Company Complex. It is good to know that the wollen industry, founded in Buckfast centuries ago by the Cistercians, continues to survive.

BIBLIOGRAPHY

Brayshay, M. 'Plymouth's Defences in the Year of the Armada' *Transactions of the Devonshire Association*, Vol. 119, 1987.
Buckfast Abbey Chronicle, 1941–42.
Crossing, W. *One Hundred Years on Dartmoor*, Devon Books, 1987.

The Dartmoor Visitor, 1990 (see 'The Past Revealed' by Deborah Griffiths).
Graf, Dom Ernest. *Anscar Vonier.*
Harris, Helen. *Industrial Archaeology of Dartmoor*, David & Charles, 1968.
Stephan, Dom John. *Buckfast Abbey.*